WHAT THE DEVIL DOESN'T WANT YOU TO KNOW

Greg Laurie

A publication of

Riverside, California
www.harvest.org

What the Devil Doesn't Want You to Know,
Revised Edition.

Copyright © 1992 by Greg Laurie. All rights reserved.
Revised Edition 2008.

Design: Harvest Design
Typesetting: Harvest Design
Copywriting: Harvest Publications
Copyediting: Harvest Publications

Printed in the United States of America.

ISBN: 978-1-932778-08-3

Visit Harvest Ministries' award-winning Web site at www.harvest.org.

CONTENTS

CHAPTER ONE:
What the Devil Doesn't Want You to Know

It is my firm conviction that we are living in the last days. By that, I mean that Bible prophecies are being fulfilled, and, as a result, Jesus Christ could come back at any time. These are dark days we are living in, but God is truly at work.

Unfortunately, God is not the only one at work right now. The devil is hard at work as well. You might not think such a being as the devil exists, but I can assure you, he does exist, and he is the mortal enemy of all humanity!

It's also obvious to me that this enemy is stepping up his efforts. Satan has become far more blatant and not nearly as subtle as he used to be. Yet, at the same time, there is also a powerful moving of God's Spirit.

We need to wake up and realize that we are living in strategic and critical times. As the apostle Paul wrote to the church in Rome,

And do this, knowing the time, that now it is high time to awake out of sleep; for now our salvation is nearer than when we first believed. The night is far spent, the day is at hand. Therefore let us cast off the works of darkness, and let us put on the armor of light. (Romans 13:12)

Paul makes it clear that these are not times for playing games with God and living with a half-hearted commitment to Him. What is the only way to survive spiritually in today's world? We must be completely committed to Jesus Christ. Otherwise, we are going to be sitting ducks for the tactics, strategies, and flaming arrows of the devil.

We need to have a realistic concept of who this spirit-being that we call "Satan" really is. On one hand, we do not want to underestimate the devil. He is a sly and skillful foe. After all, he's been perfecting his craft for over thousands of years of dealings with humankind, and he has the tricks of his trade well honed. On the other hand, we do not want to overstate his capabilities. We need to look at him rationally and understand exactly who he is and what we are dealing with.

I'm going to share with you a few things I think the devil doesn't want you to know.

CHAPTER TWO:
Satan's Power Is Limited

First on the list is the fact that Satan has definite limitations. Satan has been granted power, and it is more power than has been given to any person, but the power is restricted.

The devil would love for us to think he is the equal of God; that as God rules from heaven, the devil rules from hell; that whatever God can accomplish, the devil can, too; and that they are equals, fighting over the souls of people. That simply is not true.

God certainly does rule from heaven, but the devil does not rule from hell. The devil has not even been to hell yet, and he is far from being God's equal.

We have all seen caricatures or cartoons in which the devil is seated on a big, fiery throne in the midst of hell's flames. All the little demons with their horns and pitchforks report in each day, receive their orders, and head out into the world to do his bidding.

This is frightening, ominous, and completely false. Satan's power is limited, and he knows it. But he doesn't want you to know.

Satan Is Not Omniscient

Satan is not God's equal, not by any stretch of the imagination. Satan is not omniscient, or all-knowing. His knowledge is incomplete. Satan desires for us to think he is all-knowing; and although he is clever and has more knowledge than mere mortals, he certainly does not have unlimited knowledge.

In contrast, God knows everything about you. God knows what you're going to think before you think it. He knows where you're going before you leave to get there. He knows the future better than you and I know the past.

Satan Is Not Omnipresent

Furthermore, Satan is not omnipresent, or everywhere at the same time. Satan can only be at one place at one time. He does, however, give the impression of being everywhere because of a very well organized structure of demons under his control.

Unlike Satan, God is omnipresent, and wherever we go, God is there.

Satan Is Not Omnipotent

Satan's power is limited by the will of God in the life of the believer. That truth has very dangerous implications for you if you are not a believer. If you have not made a personal commitment to Jesus Christ and are not maintaining a proper relationship with Him right now, Satan's power is unlimited in your life. He can do whatever he wants.

Maybe you like to think that you are the master of your destiny, the captain of your ship, but in reality, you are a puppet. Satan is pulling the strings in your life.

The Bible says in 2 Corinthians 4:4, "the god of this age [the devil] has blinded [the minds], who do not believe," and the nonbelievers are taken captive to do Satan's will! As this verse clearly states, Satan is definitely powerful. But what Satan doesn't want you to know is that his power is limited.

CHAPTER THREE:
Satan Is Real

Have you ever noticed that most people who think they are in charge of their own lives all seem to be moving in the same direction? That is because they are following a pied piper, and he is whispering the same thoughts into their minds.

Satan is able to activate impulses inside them, and they are obeying him faithfully, all the time believing that he does not even exist. It is a great strategy; it has worked with brilliance and great effectiveness for thousands of years.

One of the devil's greatest deceptions is to make people think he does not exist. People envision the cartoon devil with horns, tail, hooves, and pitchfork. They laugh it off. Meanwhile, he says, "Laugh all you want. I'll see you in hell."

However, Satan's power is limited by the will of God. This is clearly illustrated in a conversation between God and Satan as recorded in the first chapter of Job. One day in heaven, a group of angels came before the Lord, and Satan was among them. God said to Satan, " 'Where have you come from?' " (verse 7 NLT).

Satan replied, " 'I have been going back and forth across the earth, watching everything that's going on' " (verse 7 NLT).

So God asked Satan a question, " 'Have you noticed my servant Job? He is the finest man in all the earth—a man of complete integrity. He fears God and will have nothing to do with evil' " (verse 8 NLT).

God was bragging about Job, just as a proud parent brags about his child. In essence, the devil's response was this, "Let me have a few days with Job. Let me have my way with his life. Then we will see what he is made of."

This troubles me when I read it, by the way. I think, *Lord, if you are proud of me, please don't brag about it.*

Satan answered God and said, "Yes, Job fears God, but not without good reason! You have always protected him and his home and his property from harm" (verses 9–10).

This was accurate. God had protected Job, and Satan could not touch Job's person or possessions without God's permission. Of course, that is true of any believer.

We all know that God allowed tragedy to befall Job. At the same time, God knew what Job could handle; He knew his breaking point. God also knows what you can handle. He knows what your vulnerabilities are. And He knows what your breaking point is.

In the upper room on the night of the last supper, Jesus leaned over and said to Simon Peter, " 'Simon, Simon! Indeed, Satan has asked for you … ' " (Luke 22:31). I think Peter started to shake in his sandals!

Then Jesus essentially said, "Not only has Satan been asking for you, but he has been asking again and again that you be taken out of the care and protection of God." Now Peter was really shaking.

Then Jesus said, " 'But I have prayed for you, that your faith should not fail ….' " (Luke 22:32). What confidence that must have brought to a badly shaken Simon! What confidence Jesus' words give me!

If I had to go out there and fight the devil in my own strength, I'd be completely destroyed. I am no match for him; nor are you. We stand in the strength of God. We stand on what He has done for us at the cross. We stand in the knowledge that Jesus is praying for us. He will not let the enemy overwhelm us! I count on God to protect me every day. If I hear a knock at the door, I ask, "Who is it?"

"It's the devil."

"Lord, would you mind getting the door?" I am not going to answer the door! "You get it, Lord. You know my weaknesses."

Yes, the devil does indeed exist, and he is a formidable foe. But he doesn't want you to know that.

Satan Has Been Defeated

Another thing the devil does not want us to know is that he has been conquered at the cross of Calvary. 1 John 3:8 says, "For this purpose the Son of God was manifested, that He might destroy the works of the devil."

Satan knows that! Ever since he first began deceiving and tempting humankind, the devil has known that Jesus Christ would destroy him and all his works. God told him then that His Son, the Son of God, would "crush your head" (Genesis 3:15 NLT).

Satan knows he has been defeated, but he doesn't want you to know it.

CHAPTER FOUR:
Satan Is Strategic

What are some of the most commonly used strategies of this already-defeated adversary? It may surprise you to find that he moves in predictable patterns, using the same successful tactics over and over again. I suppose he operates under the philosophy, "If it ain't broke, don't fix it." He has found that these strategies have worked, so why change them?

Victor Hugo once said, "A good general must penetrate the brain of his enemy." We need to know what the enemy has in mind. The apostle Paul tells us we are not ignorant of Satan's devices, meaning that we are not ignorant of the schemes, plans, strategies, and tricks of the devil (see 2 Corinthians 2:11).

Satan is a dangerous wolf who often disguises himself as a sheep. Sometimes he will come on like a lion, but more often he sneaks in like a snake. Sometimes, he appears in all of his depravity and horror. Other times, he disguises himself as an angel of light. You may be resisting him on one hand and setting up housekeeping with him on the other! When Satan attacks, he utilizes seven primary strategies:

1. A Blatant Frontal Attack
2. Subtle Infiltration
3. Counterfeits
4. Doubt
5. Tolerance
6. Temptation
7. Deception

Strategy Number One: Frontal Attack

In attacking the early church, Satan's first thought was that by physical persecution, he could snuff out the tiny group of believers in Jerusalem. He bombarded them with harassment and persecution, and in doing so, he accomplished great things for the cause of the gospel!

The church knew that Jesus was someone worth believing in, and harassment caused them to cling more tightly to each other and to God. They trusted God for His power, and when persecution hit, they simply spread out and went everywhere preaching the Word.

Instead of wrecking the church, persecution strengthened it. Much to the devil's disgust, the church became a "lean, mean, preaching machine."

As Satan watched this, he realized that this tactic was not working, but he thought he had an ace up his sleeve. He still had his main man: Saul of Tarsus. Saul had been responsible for the death of the first martyr of the church, a courageous young man named Stephen (see Acts 22:19–20). Saul was out there doing the devil's bidding and Satan was clearly on a roll.

Then things even got worse for the devil. One day, on the Damascus Road, Saul came to know Jesus Christ (see Acts 9:1–7). He was transformed from Saul of Tarsus, to Paul the apostle. Instead of being a man driven by hate, he became a man motivated by love, and one of the most powerful preachers in the new church. What a blow to the forces of darkness! And what a victory for the kingdom of God!

Strategy Number Two: Infiltration

Satan reasoned, "Hmmm … back to the drawing board. This frontal attack isn't working as well as I had hoped. I am actually helping these Christians."

His next move was a shrewd one. He decided it was time to go undercover and infiltrate.

There was a time in church history when, almost overnight, believers went from hiding in the catacombs to living in the palaces. This occurred when the Roman Emperor Constantine claimed to be converted and stopped oppressing the church. Being a confessed believer himself, he elevated Christians from persecution to a place of prominence. They literally went from rags to riches, practically overnight.

The Christians' new respectability seriously weakened them. Compromise set in. Charles Colson has pointed out that history repeatedly shows us the church either being persecuted or corrupted. This is the result of Satan's tactic of infiltration.

G. Campbell Morgan said, "The Church persecuted has always been the Church pure. The Church patronized has always been the Church impure."

The devil may confront you in a blatant outward attack: maybe an enticement to do evil; maybe a temptation to become sexually permissive, to be unfaithful to your spouse; to dabble in drugs or alcohol; to steal or lie.

When he uses such overt tactics, you're well aware that he's at work. "I'm not going to give in to that," you smile to yourself. So he'll come to you more subtly and say, "Let's work out a compromise. Go ahead and go to church if you want to. Go ahead and read the Bible and pray. Just lower your standards a little bit here and there. We'll get along just fine. You do not need to go to church so often, and there are other things to read besides the Bible. Take it easy. Kick back. Do it later. *Mañana*."

Through compromise and infiltration, he can immobilize and sterilize you. Satan's infiltration of the church has proved to be his most effective method.

Strategy Number Three: Counterfeits

Jesus told the parable of a man who sowed wheat. In the night, an enemy came and sowed tares among the wheat.

A tare, which grows from a darnel seed, is a plant that looks exactly like a stalk of wheat as it begins to grow. Ultimately, it outgrows and uproots the wheat.

Satan has flooded the market with counterfeits and imitations. There are so many frauds out there that a lot of nonbelievers say, "Forget it. I don't even want to deal with it. I go to catch a plane at the airport and eight people come up to me from different religious persuasions, trying to convert me. They are all out of their minds. I don't want to hear about any of it."

If that is a person's reaction, it is clear that the devil's strategy has succeeded.

By sowing tares among the wheat, he causes some people to mistakenly throw the baby out with the bathwater. They do not take the time to consider the truth, because they are so frustrated by all the imitations.

You can see how well this deception has worked. Satan has pretenders in the pews and predators in the pulpits. He even has a counterfeit gospel.

As the apostle Paul told the early Christians in Galatia, "But even if we, or an angel from heaven, preach any other gospel than what we have preached to you, let him be accursed" (Galatians 1:8). Similarly, Paul pointed out to the believers in Corinth that "Satan can disguise himself as an angel of light" (2 Corinthians 11:14 NLT).

It is not surprising if his servants also disguise themselves as servants of righteousness. In the last days,

Satan is even going to have a counterfeit Christ who will present himself as a great leader who apparently has all the answers. This man of peace will be called the Antichrist: the coming world leader.

Strategy Number Four: Doubt

Satan has been in business for a long, long time. To understand just how long, you need to go back to the first book of the Bible and take a look at Genesis 3:1–7. In this foundational chapter, we can see the wiles the devil used on Adam and Eve; I think you will notice that they are precisely the same ones he is practicing on us today:

> Now the serpent was more cunning than any beast of the field which the Lord God had made. And he said to the woman, "Has God indeed said, 'You shall not eat of every tree of the garden'?" And the woman said to the serpent, "We may eat the fruit of the trees of the garden; but of the fruit of the tree which is in the midst of the garden, God has said, 'You shall not eat it, nor shall you touch it, lest you die.'" Then the serpent said to the woman, "You will not surely die. For God knows that in the day you eat of it your eyes will be opened, and you will be like God, knowing good and evil." So when the woman saw that the tree was good for food, that it was pleasant to the eyes, and a tree desirable to make one wise, she took of its fruit and ate. She also gave to her husband with her, and he ate. Then the eyes of both of them were opened, and they knew that they were naked; and they sewed fig leaves together and made themselves coverings.

In this passage, we can see Satan's strategy working. He convinced Eve to doubt the Word of God, and she fell into sin, disobeying God. We need always to remember that the Word of God is true and it is eternal, and we need to obey His Word.

Strategy Number Five: Tolerance

Do you recognize the basic principles of a satanic attack? When Satan wanted to lead the first man and woman into sin, he started by attacking the mind. The apostle Paul reminds us of this in 2 Corinthians 11:3, "I fear, lest somehow, as the serpent deceived Eve by his craftiness, your minds may be led astray from the simplicity and purity that is in Christ."

The human mind is incredibly vulnerable and impressionable. It is in the mind that we reason, contemplate, and allow our imaginations free rein. That is why the Bible encourages us with these words:

> For the weapons of our warfare are not carnal but mighty in God for pulling down strongholds, casting down arguments and every high thing that exalts itself against the knowledge of God, bringing every thought into captivity to the obedience of Christ. (2 Corinthians 10:4–5)

When you daydream, contemplate, or think about things that are harmful spiritually, you have taken the first step toward doing those things.

Today, some of the things we once considered taboo and would not even speak about are now commonly discussed; they are joked about on television sitcoms; they are made light of in print, in movies, and in music.

This familiarity constitutes the first step toward a change in human behavior. Public acceptance convinces us that maybe certain actions are not so bad after all.

It's the same in our personal lives. We may not respond to some blatantly obvious temptation. If the devil were to come to you and say, "I've got a great idea! I want you to think about this: why don't you have an affair with your secretary? Then, end your marriage in divorce and watch your children be estranged from you. Why not allow your whole family to fall apart? Ultimately, you can turn to alcohol and die prematurely. What do you think? Shall we start right away?"

Your obvious response to such a blatant approach would be: "Get serious. Do you think I'm a fool? I would never do that."

Of course, the devil knows this. So, he comes to you with a different tactic. He subtly suggests, "Wouldn't it be fun if you just dreamed a little? Of course, you will never act on it. Just think about it. Take a trip to fantasy island."

So you start thinking about it, toying with it in your imagination. Then, no longer satisfied with just fantasizing about it, you start flirting a little bit with someone other than your wife or husband. It's nothing serious, of course, just an innocent lunch together.

Then, one thing leads to another and the next thing you know, you are in serious trouble. You say, "How could this have happened? I cannot believe I fell into such an obvious trap!"

The Bible directs you not to give a foothold to the devil. But you did, when you allowed yourself to tolerate the idea of improper behavior.

Strategy Number Six: Temptation

Temptation usually starts in the realm of our minds. It has been said, "You cannot stop a bird from flying over your head, but you can stop him from building a nest in your hair." That means I cannot prevent an impure thought from passing by, but I can keep it from becoming the center of my thoughts.

It is not a sin to be tempted. It is a sin to give in to temptation.

We have all been assaulted by impure thoughts. They often come at the worst times. You may be in church, reading the Bible, or singing a praise song when some devious, bizarre, sinful thought comes into your mind. Then the devil says, "How could you think such a thing? You call yourself a Christian?"

Temptation is one of the oldest tricks in the book. That is why we should bring every thought into captivity to the obedience of Christ.

The next time Satan brings up that sinful thought, remind yourself, "I didn't come up with that, and I am not going to think about it. It is evil and impure, and I don't want anything to do with it."

The apostle John said, "For all that is in the world—the lust of the flesh, the lust of the eyes, and the pride of life—is not of the Father but is of the world" (1 John 2:16). John's words here basically break down the three categories of temptation.

1. The lust of the flesh
2. The lust of the eyes
3. The pride of life

A person who has fallen into the lust of desires of the flesh is basically a person who gives into his or her impulses.

I have a dog that does pretty much whatever he wants to do. When he feels like taking a nap, he collapses. When he gets hungry, he goes and rustles up something. If he feels the urge to do something else, he does it. He just gives in to whatever his impulses are.

There are people like that. They just live to gratify their cravings and desires. They serve the lust of the flesh.

The lust of the eyes is mental temptation: what we see, contemplate, think about, and fantasize over. Sin often begins here.

The pride of life is more subtle. You might be a person who does not indulge in other sinful activities. You live a moral life. You have a fine family. You work hard, with honesty, and enjoy a good career. You are pursuing excellence and knowledge. You might even be a religious person. You might be patting yourself on the back saying, "I am so wonderful. I am so moral. I am so good. I am so intelligent. Best of all, I am so humble."

You can be deceived by the pride of life. Egotism and pride are as much a deception as the lust of the flesh or the lust of the eyes.

Bearing in mind these three ideas—the lust of the flesh, the lust of the eyes, and the pride of life—let's see if we can find them in Eve's temptation in the garden.

Genesis 3:6 tells us that Eve "saw that the tree … was good for food." There it is—the lust of the flesh. Then the Bible tells us that she saw that it "was pleasant to the eyes." There it is   the lust of the eyes. Then she saw that it was "desirable to make one wise." Finally, we have the pride of life.

There you have it: Eve gave in to the temptation. The enemy will hit you in those three areas over and over again.

Strategy Number Seven: Deception

The Word also teaches us that one of the foundational strategies of the devil is lying. Revelation 12:9 says he is the "serpent of old, called the Devil and Satan, who deceives the whole world." Referring to Satan's lying nature, Jesus said " 'There is no truth in him … for he is a liar and the father of lies' " (John 8:44 NLT).

The first way Satan deceives us is by questioning God's Word. We see Satan lying to Eve in the garden. First of all, he questioned God's Word. He was so cunning! In Genesis 3:1, Satan asked Eve, "Has God indeed said, 'You shall not eat of every tree in the garden'?"

Satan did not deny that God had spoken. He simply questioned whether God had really said what Eve had thought He had said.

He implied, "God does not really love you, Eve. If God really loved you, He would let you eat of any tree that appealed to you. Therefore, when He says you cannot eat of this tree, He is holding something back from you that you really need to look into." He questioned the Word of God.

Satan will also do that in the life of the believer. He will say to us, "Do you really believe the Bible is the Word of God? Do you really think you are saved? You are not saved. God has not forgiven you. You do not deserve it. Look at you. Look at that sin you just committed. You call yourself a Christian? Don't even think of going to church. That would be the ultimate hypocrisy. Stay home and watch television instead. Don't you dare pray. God will not listen to you. Forget about reading the Bible, because God will not speak to you through the Bible anyway, after what you have done."

You say, "Thanks, devil, that's great advice." Don't believe him. He's a liar!

When you sin, you have all the more reason to pray and ask God to forgive you. When you sin, you have all the more reason to go to church and get help and support from your Christian friends. When you sin, it is vital that you read the Word of God to see what it has to say to you. Then, apply what you read and act decisively on it.

Don't base your salvation on the way you feel, but on what God has said. God said through the apostle John, "These things I have written to you who believe in the name of the Son of God, that *you may know that you have eternal life*" (1 John 5:13, emphasis mine). Now that is something to hang on to! Memorize that and remind yourself of it when you are going through times of struggle.

Satan's second form of deception comes through denying God's Word. First, Satan questioned God's Word. Then in verse 4, he said, " 'You will not surely die.' "

It is but a short step from questioning the Word of God to denying it. If Eve had not listened to Satan questioning God's Word, she would never have fallen.

That is why the Bible says in James 4:7, "Resist the devil and he will flee from you." Eve fell into the devil's trap, because she talked to the devil. Don't talk to him! Satan's lies are subtle.

As Alfred Tennyson said, "A lie that is all of a lie can be met with and fought outright. A lie that is partly the truth is a harder matter to fight." When Satan lies openly and blatantly, it is one thing, but when he mixes a little truth into his lies, discernment becomes more difficult.

Satan's third and final form of deception is by making substitutions for God's Word. In Genesis 3:5, Satan says, " 'You will be like God, knowing good and evil.' " In the place of God's true Word, Satan has substituted his own lie.

> First, he questioned God's Word.
> Second, he denied God's Word.
> Third, he substituted his own lie.

It's an effective strategy. We need to be on guard against false teaching and distortions of God's Word. They can only lead us astray and bring us trouble.

CHAPTER FIVE:
God Has a Plan for Victory

God has a plan for us to reach victory over the devil and his strategies. But the devil doesn't want us to know that. Let's look at what we can do to be victors with Christ.

Know God's Word

Eve had a choice to make. Should she believe the Word of God or believe the word of the devil? We know which choice she made. Eve and Adam both sinned and did what God had told them not to do.

They failed to use the weapon God has given all of us to use during times of temptation. This weapon is His Word, also known as the "sword of the Spirit."

Satan tried to deceive Jesus during His temptation in the wilderness. Satan said,

> If You are the Son of God, throw Yourself down. For it is written: "He shall give His angels charge over

you," and, "In their hands they shall bear you up, lest you dash your foot against a stone." (Matthew 4:6)

The devil knew the Bible, but he quoted it out of context. He omitted the all-important phrase, "To keep you in all your ways" (Psalm 91:11).

Someone once saw W. C. Fields reading a Bible. Amazed, the observer said, "Why are you—W. C. Fields—reading that?" In his best form, the famous comedian and skeptic replied, "Looking for loopholes … looking for loopholes … "

Satan, as a student of Scripture, does precisely the same thing. Jesus replied, " 'You shall not tempt the Lord your God' " (Matthew 4:7). He pulled out that sword of the Spirit and—*touché*! That is what we need to do. We need to know the Word of God. Then, when the enemy comes with his lies and temptations and distortions, we can use Scripture offensively and defend ourselves too.

Resist Temptation

Maybe you are wondering, "Why does God even allow temptation? Life would be so much easier if God would take all temptation away and let us cruise on through life until we get to heaven!"

Temptation, believe it or not, can have a positive impact on our lives. Temptation separates the men from the boys; women from the girls; the wheat from the chaff; the true from the false. When you are a true child of God and you are tempted, you cling to God all the more.

A. B. Simpson said,

> Temptation exercises our faith and teaches us to pray. It is like a military drill and a taste of battle to the young soldier. It puts us under fire and compels us to exercise our weapons and prove their potency. It shows us the recourse of Christ and the preciousness of the promises of God. Every victory gives us new confidence in our victorious leader and new courage for the next onslaught of the foe.

If you are not walking with the Lord, you will probably dabble with temptation. You may toy with it. If you do, you will ultimately fall into sin.

On the other hand, James 1:12 says, "Blessed is the man who endures temptation: for when he has been approved, he will receive the crown of life which the Lord has promised to those who love Him." When you resist temptation, you will grow stronger.

Let me give you a word of warning. Temptation will often hit you during times of blessing and spiritual victory. Brace yourself. Many times after God has really ministered to you or has used you, Satan will have his bow loaded with his flaming arrows, and he will nail you.

Jesus was faced with His most challenging temptation, apart from the cross, immediately after His baptism, when the Spirit of God came upon Him in the form of a dove. After the dove came the devil, tempting Him in the wilderness (see Matthew 4:1–11). Jesus was confronted by a demon-possessed person after He had been transfigured on the mountain with Moses and Elijah (see Matthew 17:14–18). It is after the blessing that buffeting and attacks often come.

Draw Near to God

We need to keep up our guard and stay as close to God as we can. The apostle James tells us to "Resist the devil and he will flee from you. Draw near to God and He will draw near to you" (James 4:7–8).

You see, the only way to effectively resist the devil is to draw near to God! Then we will have the power and resources we need to resist his enticements and temptations.

The only way to draw near to God is to come to Him through His own Son, Jesus Christ. The devil knows that, too, but he doesn't want you to know!

Jesus said, "I am the way, the truth, and the life. No one comes to the Father except through Me" (John 14:6). Jesus died on the cross for you two thousand years ago! The Bible teaches that we've all sinned and fallen short of the glory of God (Romans 3:23). Jesus took the penalty of our sin upon Himself on that dark day on Calvary's cross.

And now, if you turn from your sin and ask Him to forgive you and be your Lord and Savior, He will do just that for you!

Don't hesitate. Jesus is just a prayer away! If you would like to make that commitment to Christ, you might just pray this simple prayer:

> Lord Jesus, come into my life and forgive me of my sin as I turn from it now. Help me to draw near to You and to resist the devil. Help me also to be Your disciple. Thank You for loving me, Lord. In Jesus' name, Amen.

If you've prayed that prayer, I would love to hear from you. I also would like to send you some helpful materials, at no cost, to encourage you in your spiritual growth. Please write to me, or visit knowGod.org.

Greg Laurie
HARVEST MINISTRIES

P.O. Box 4000
Riverside, CA 92514-4000

PastorGreg@harvest.org
www.harvest.org

PASTOR GREG'S DAILY DEVOTIONS

Get Connected Today!

Sign up today for Greg Laurie's daily e-mail devotions. You'll receive daily encouragement and relevant teaching in a quick, bite-sized format during the week, plus a longer, in-depth article on the weekends.

To get Pastor Greg's daily devotions, visit harvest.org.

HARVEST TOOLS

Helping you know God and make Him known

Visit harvest-tools.org to see Harvest Ministries' entire line of booklets, books, music, tracts, Bibles, and studies–available at discount prices for churches and ministries.

To order resources from Harvest Ministries, contact us at:

Harvest Resources
6115 Arlington Ave.
Riverside CA, 92504
Phone: 951.354.1392
FAX: 951.351.8045
harvest-tools.org

NOTES

NOTES

ARE YOU PREPARED FOR THE STRATEGIES AND FLAMING ARROWS OF THE DEVIL?

In *What the Devil Doesn't Want You to Know*, Greg Laurie exposes the commonly held myths and misunderstandings surrounding the devil, clearly showing his weaknesses and limitations in the life of the believer. You'll learn scriptural truths on:

- The limitations of Satan's power
- His strategies and weaknesses
- Ways to overcome Satan
- God's plan for victory over the devil

Read *What the Devil Doesn't Want You to Know* and discover victory in Christ.

Greg Laurie pastors Harvest Christian Fellowship (one of America's largest churches) in Riverside, California. He is the author of several books, including the Gold Medallion Award winner, *The Upside-Down Church*, as well as *Every Day with Jesus* and *Wrestling with God*. You can find his study notes in the *New Believer's Bible* and the *Seeker's Bible*.

Host of the *Harvest: Greg Laurie* television program and the nationally syndicated radio program *A New Beginning*, Laurie is also the founder and featured speaker for Harvest Crusades—contemporary, large-scale evangelistic outreaches, which local churches organize nationally and internationally.

Laurie has appeared on *ABC World News Tonight*, *Fox News*, and *MSNBC*, sharing how the Bible is relevant for people today. He resides in Southern California with his wife, Cathe.

ISBN 1-932778-08-X

9 781932 778083

FOUR KEYS

TO EFFECTIVELY

YOUR FAITH

GREG LAURIE